Dedicated to
My brilliant wife, Briana
Who has good ideas

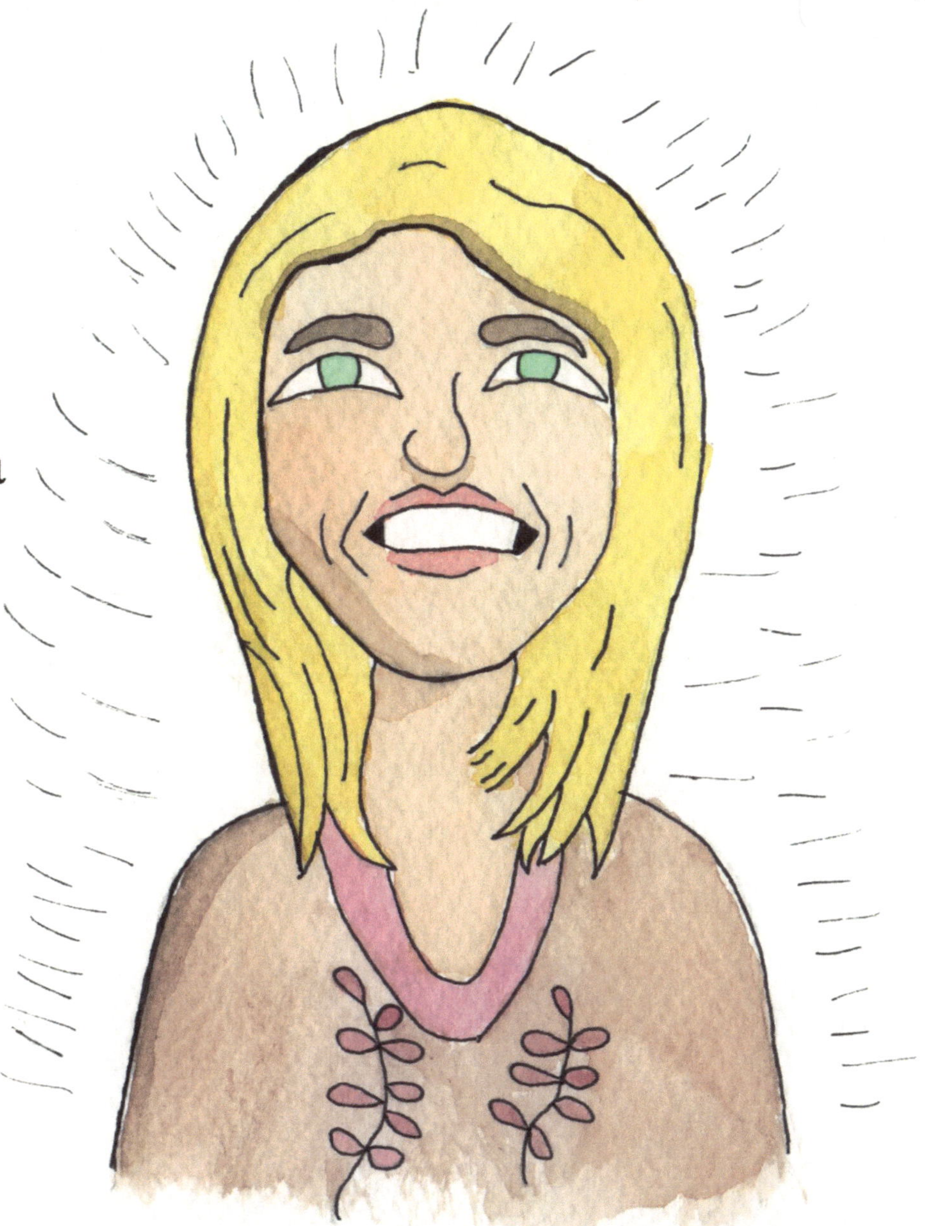

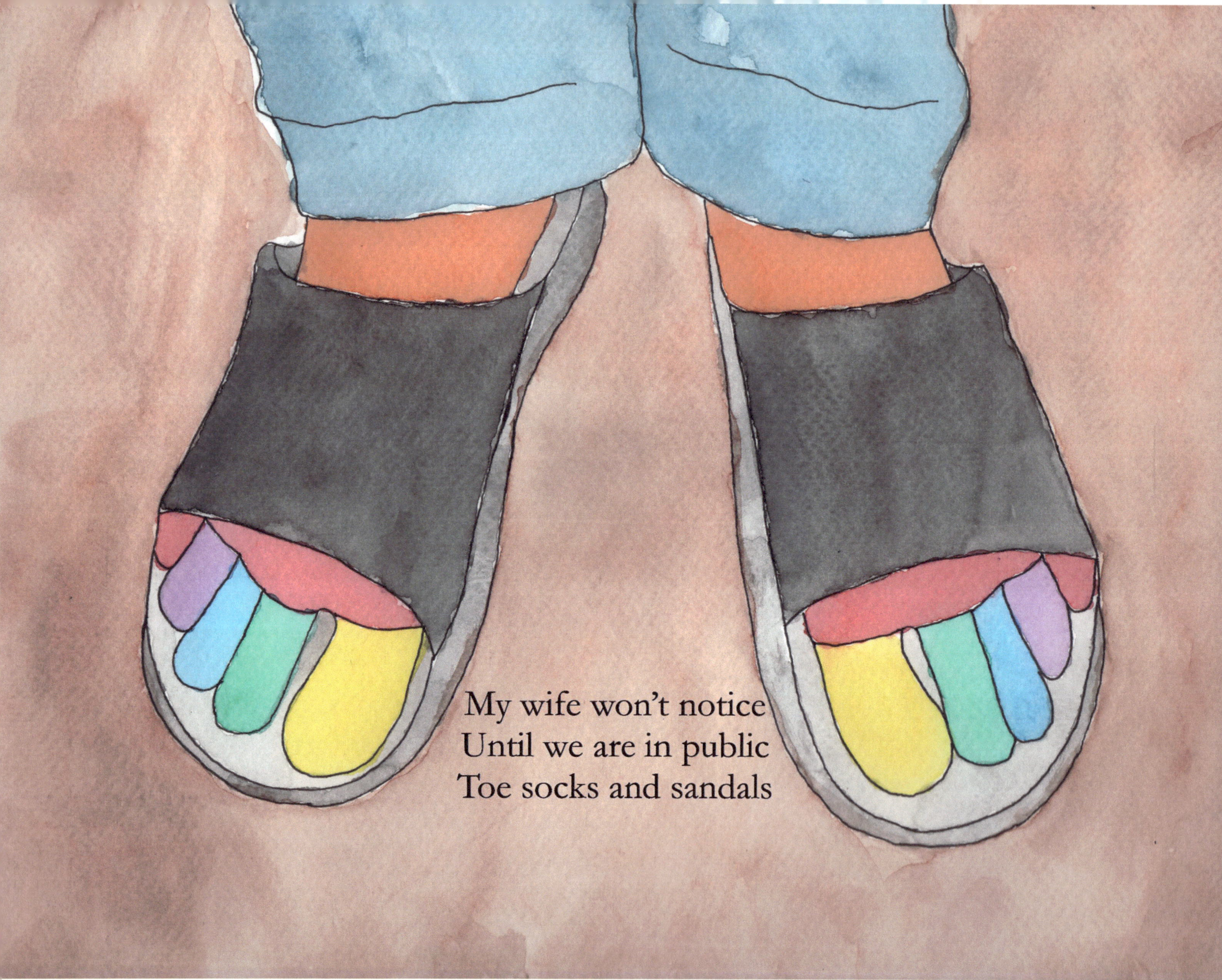
My wife won't notice
Until we are in public
Toe socks and sandals

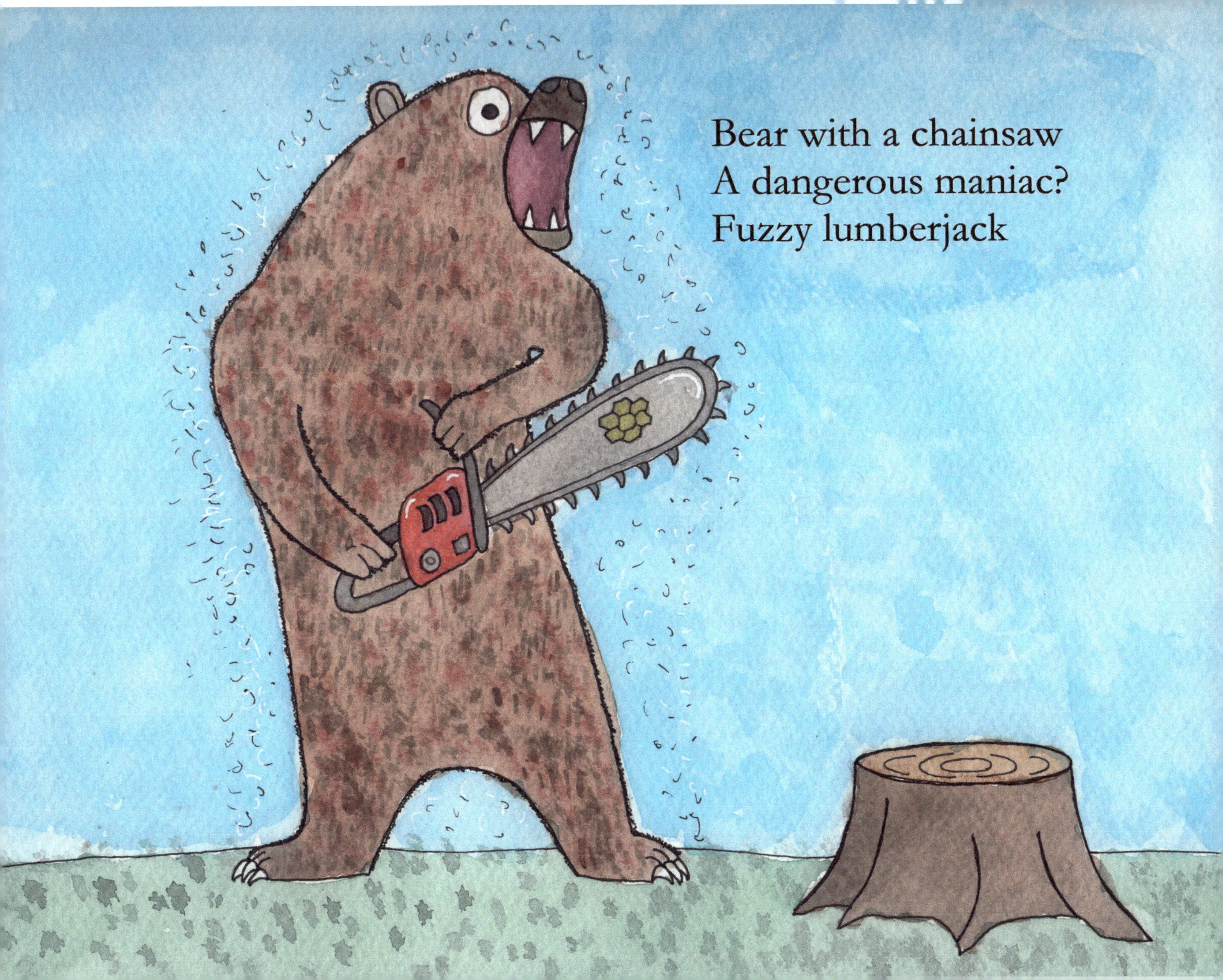

Bear with a chainsaw
A dangerous maniac?
Fuzzy lumberjack

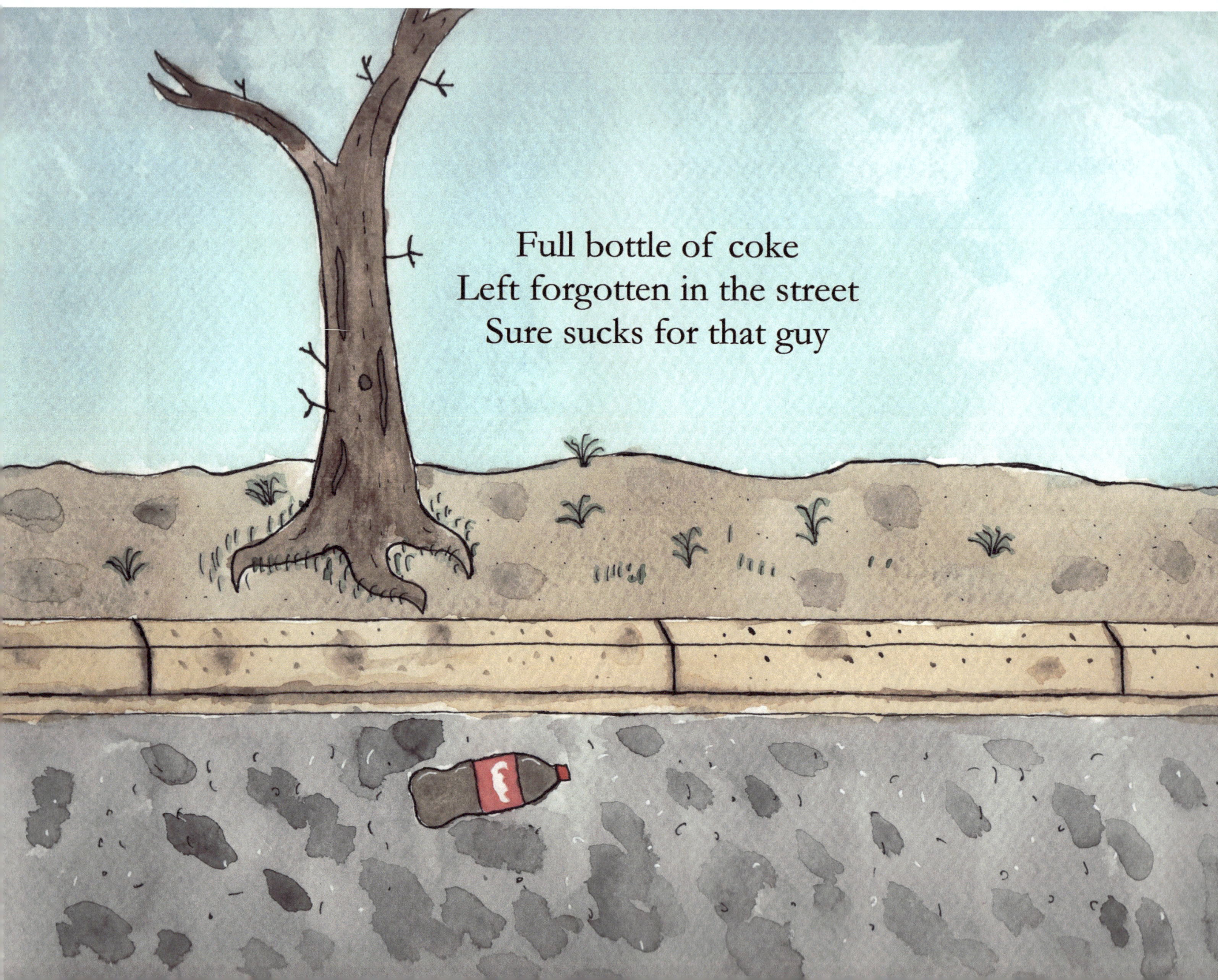

Full bottle of coke
Left forgotten in the street
Sure sucks for that guy

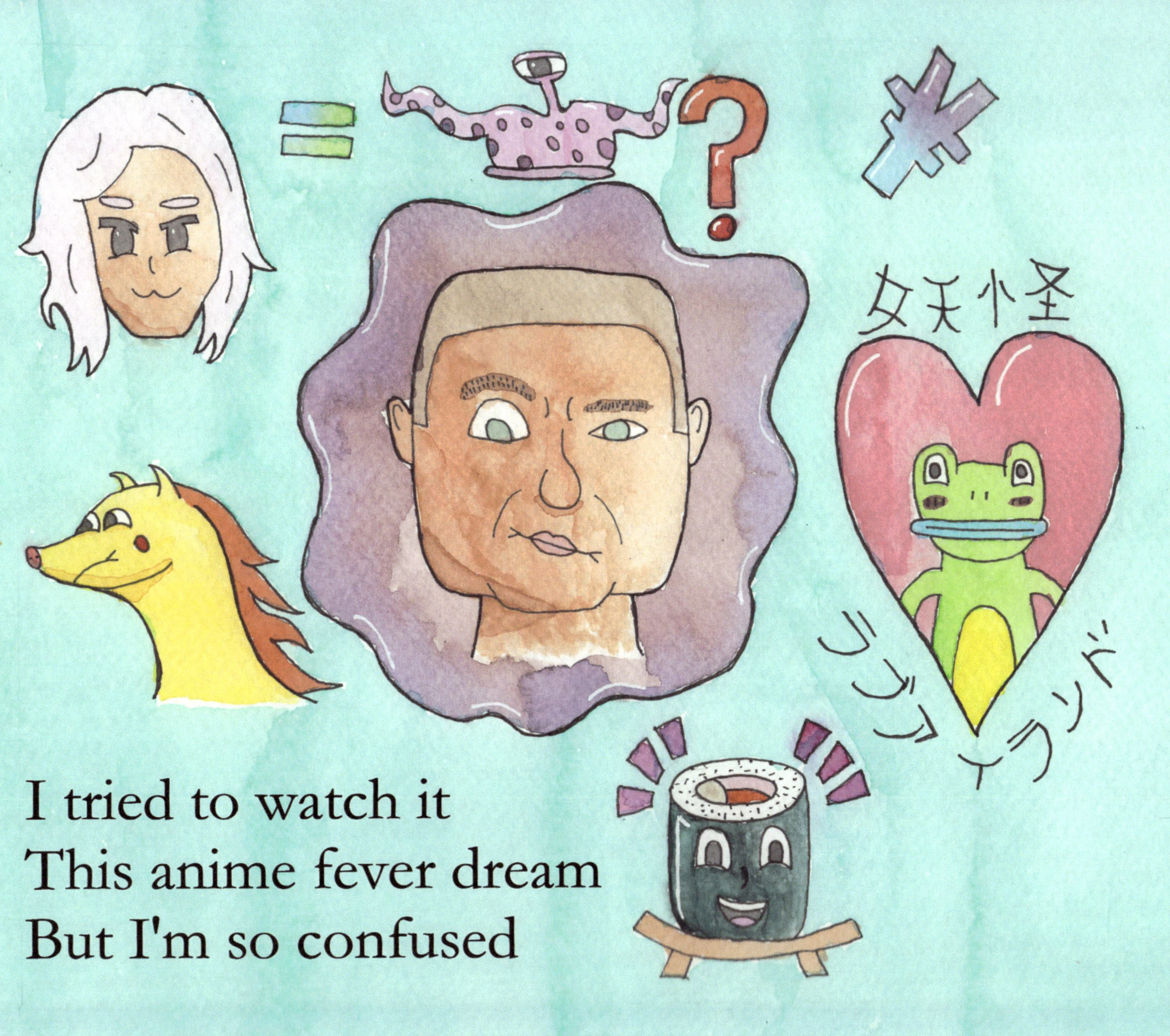
妖怪
ラブランド
I tried to watch it
This anime fever dream
But I'm so confused

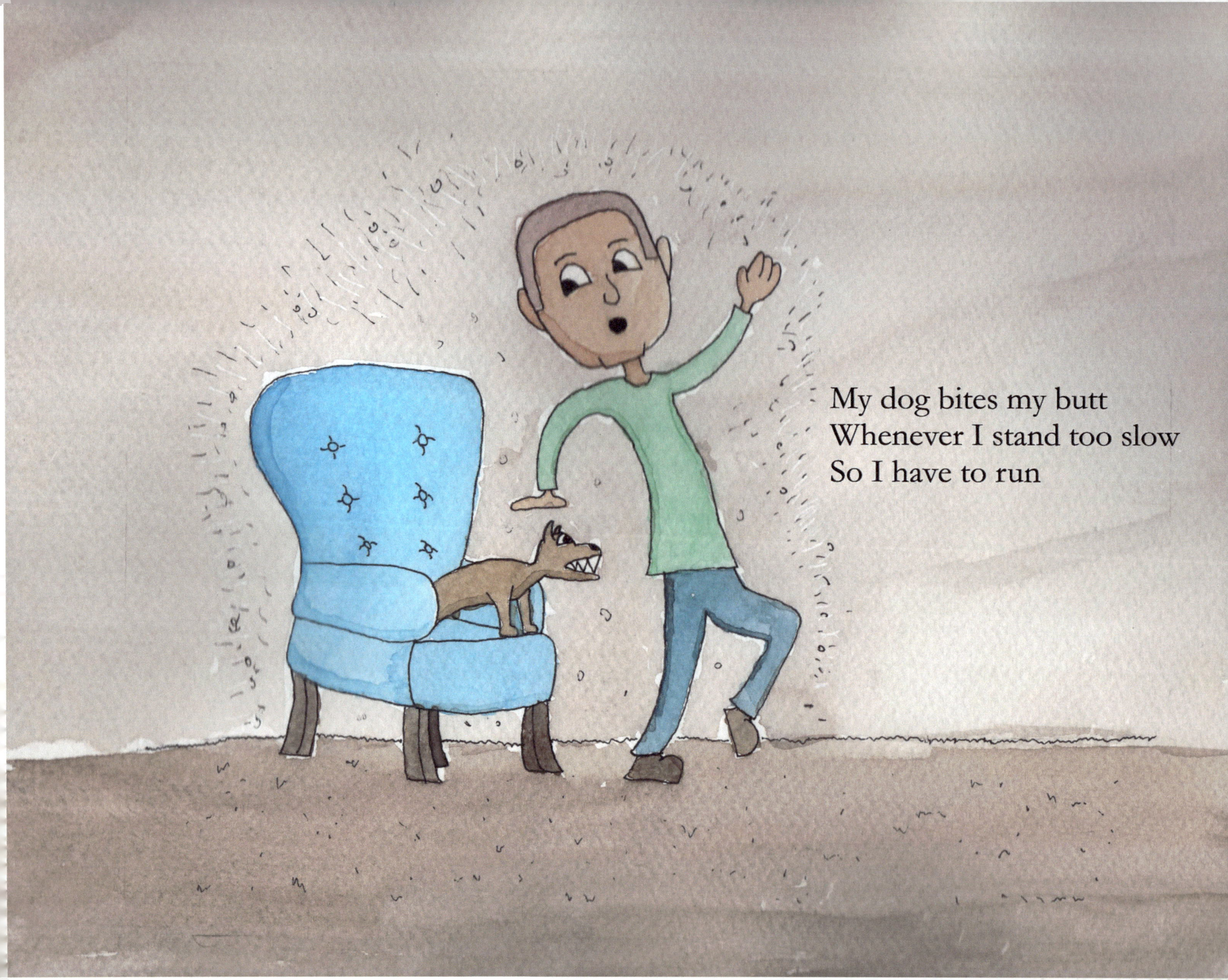
My dog bites my butt
Whenever I stand too slow
So I have to run

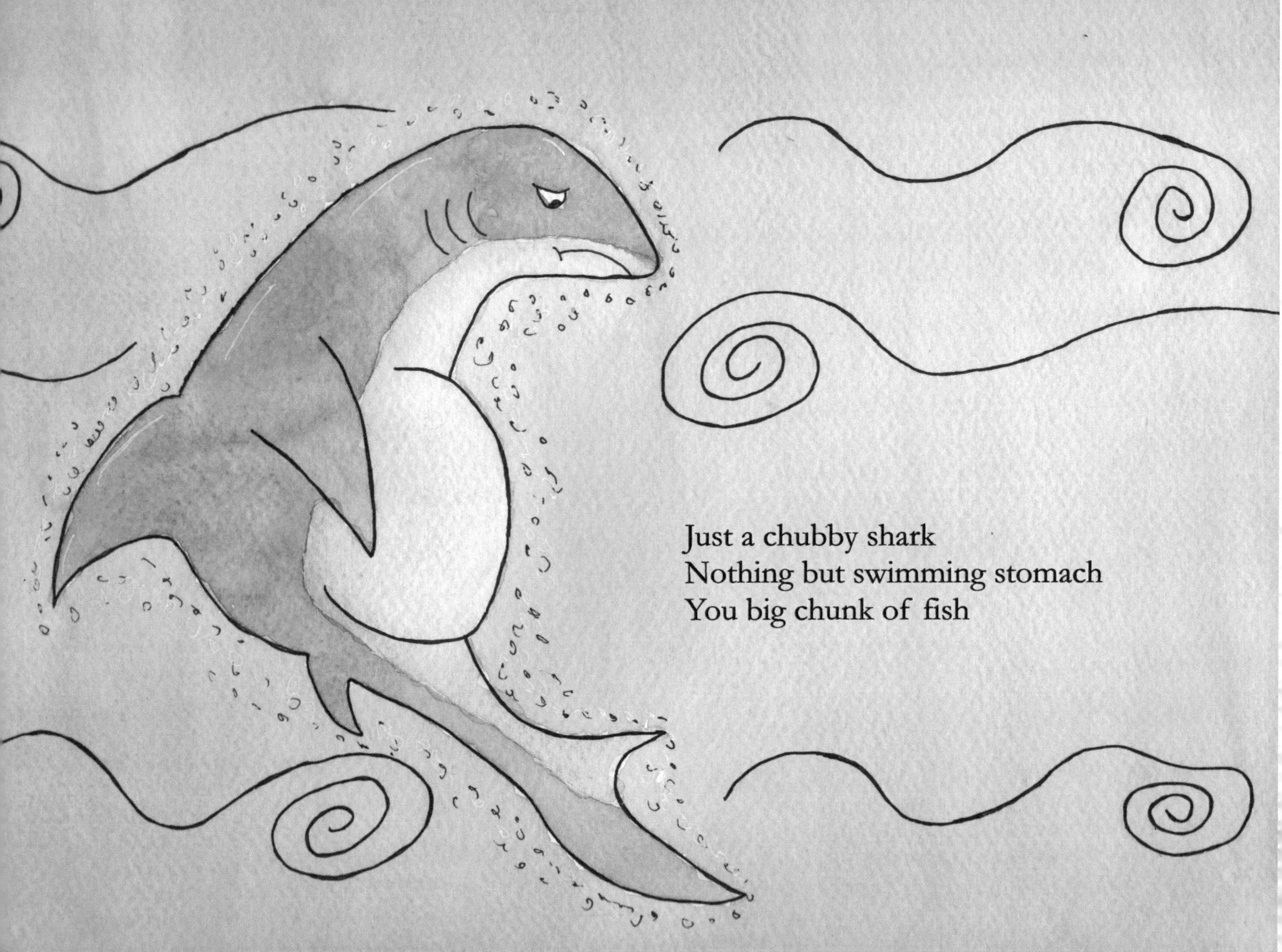


Just a chubby shark
Nothing but swimming stomach
You big chunk of fish

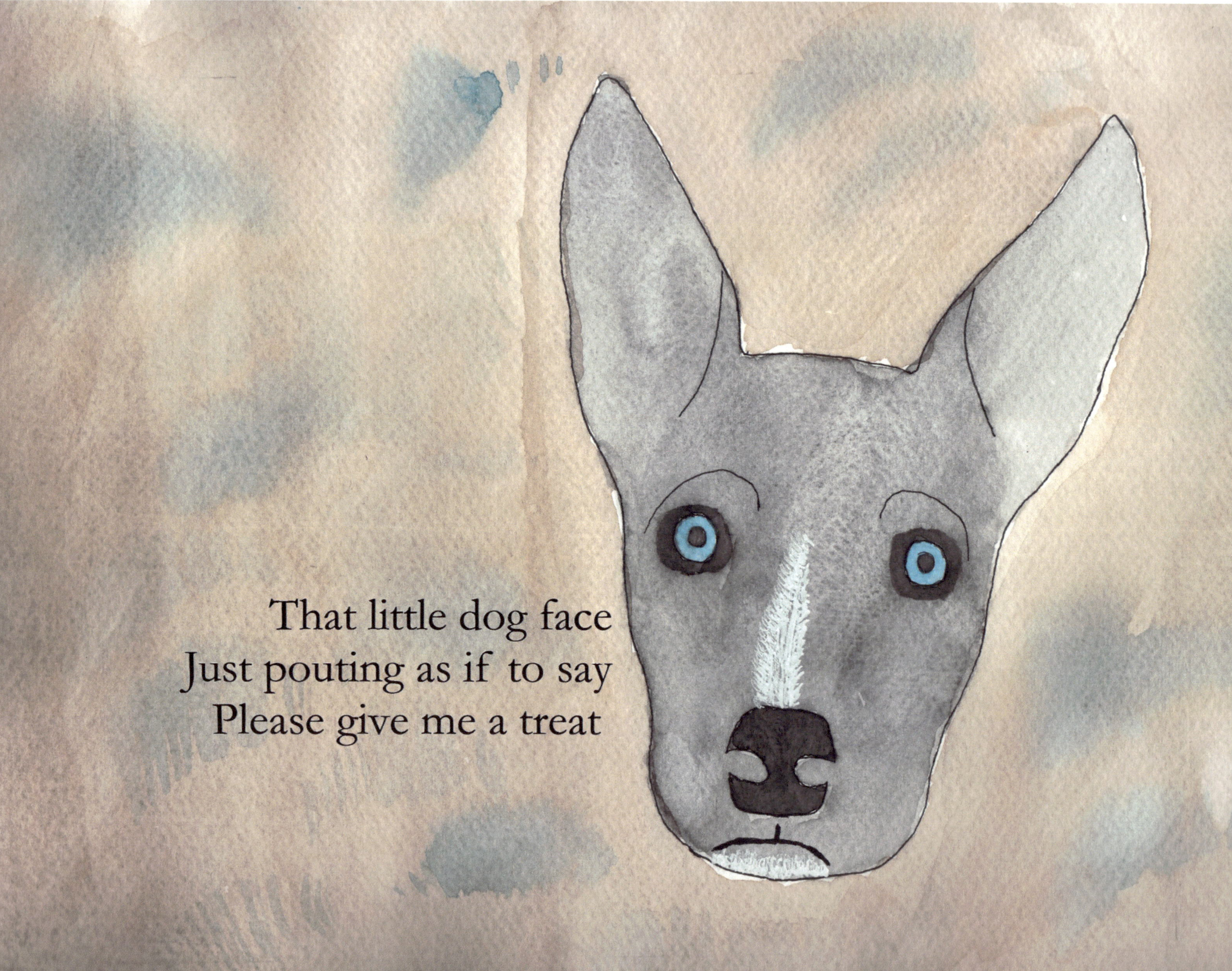

That little dog face
Just pouting as if to say
Please give me a treat

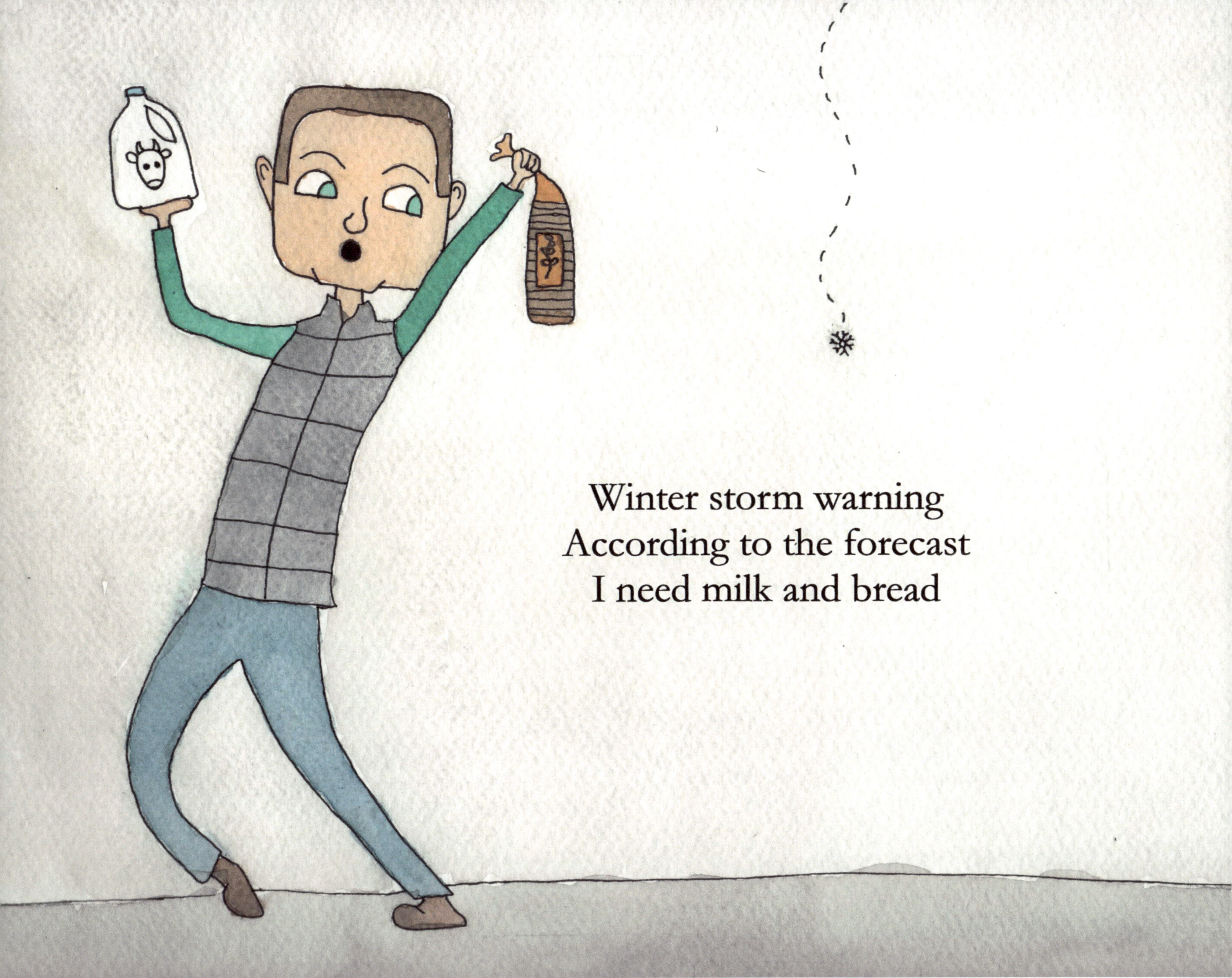

Winter storm warning
According to the forecast
I need milk and bread

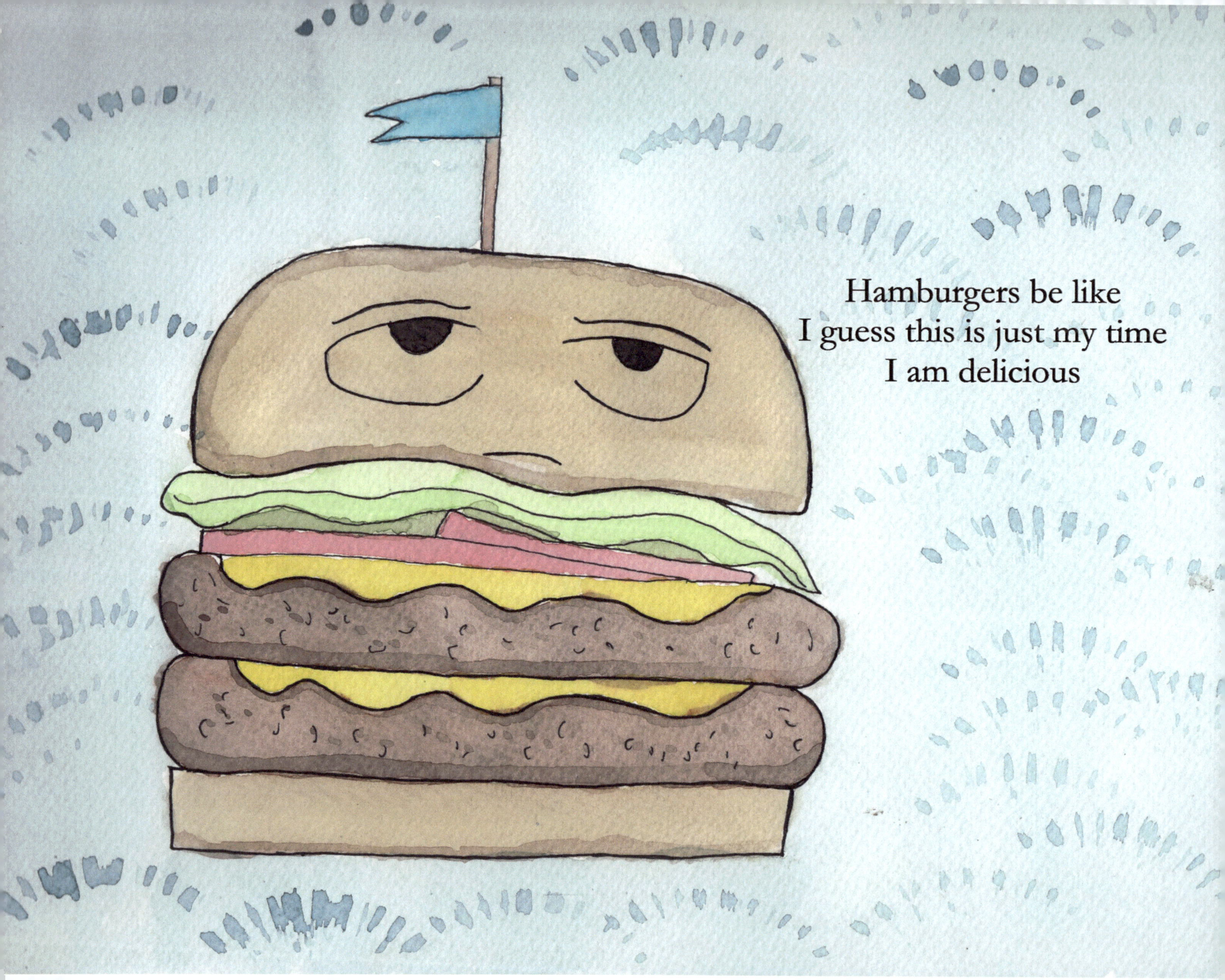

Hamburgers be like
I guess this is just my time
I am delicious

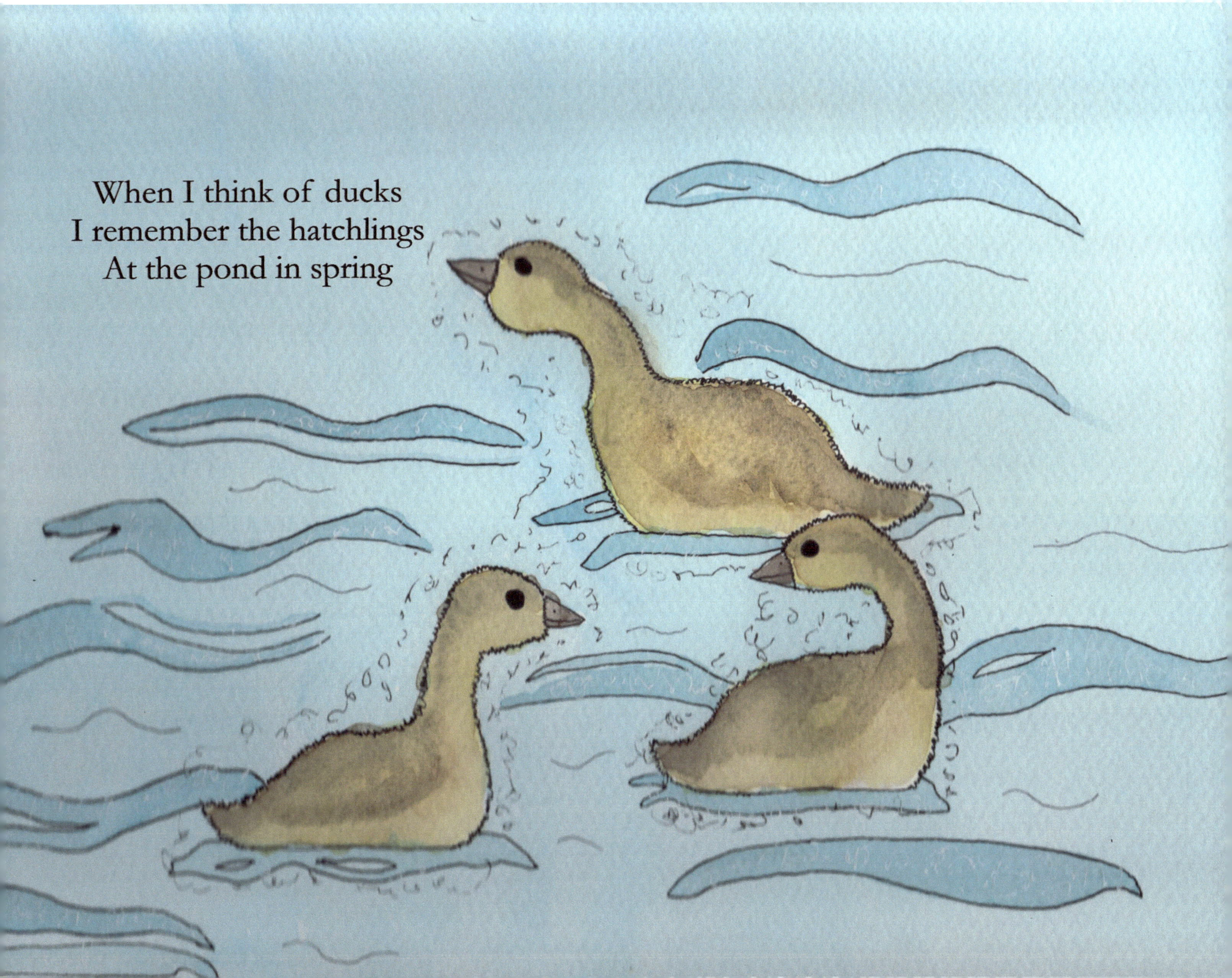

When I think of ducks
I remember the hatchlings
At the pond in spring

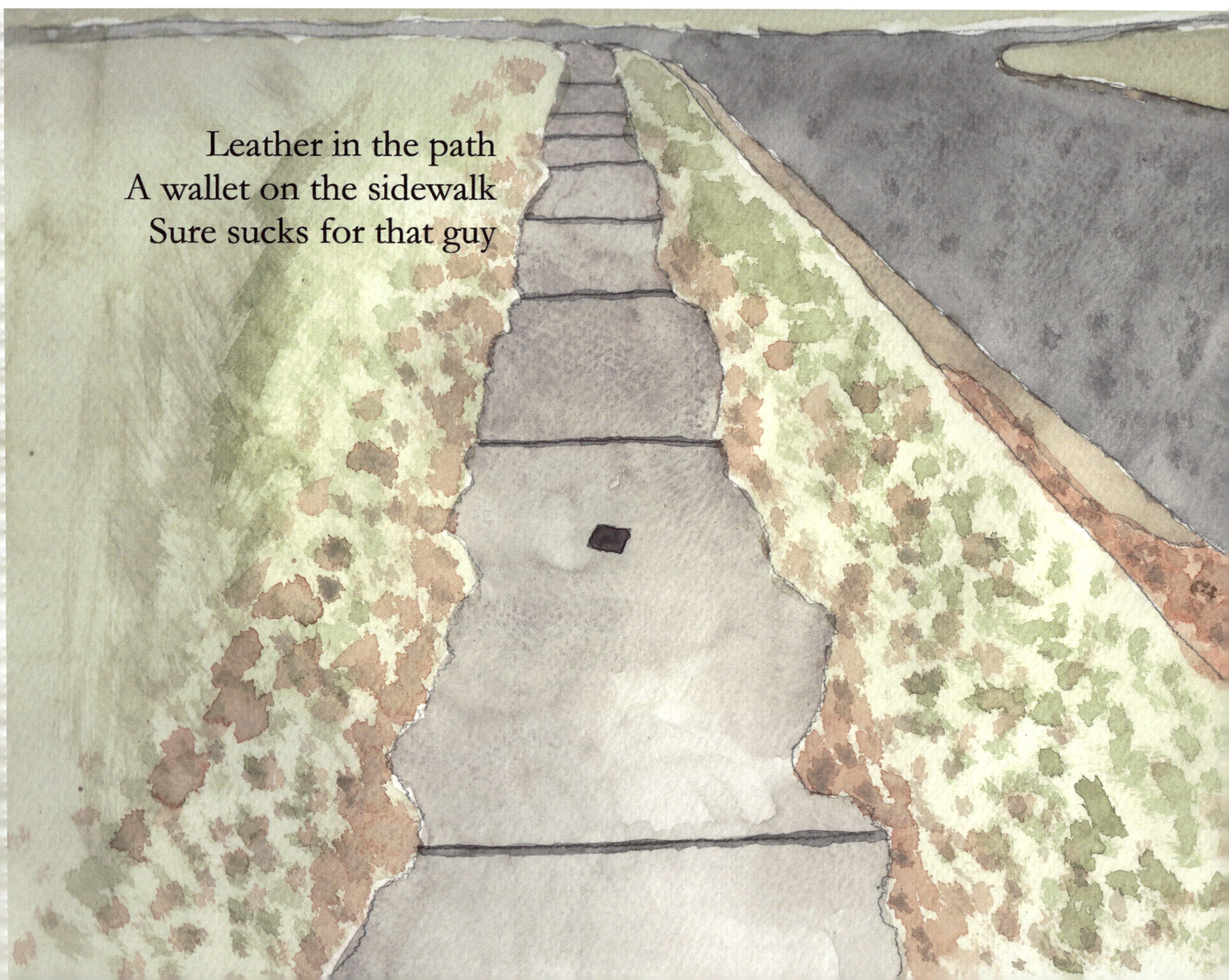

Leather in the path
A wallet on the sidewalk
Sure sucks for that guy

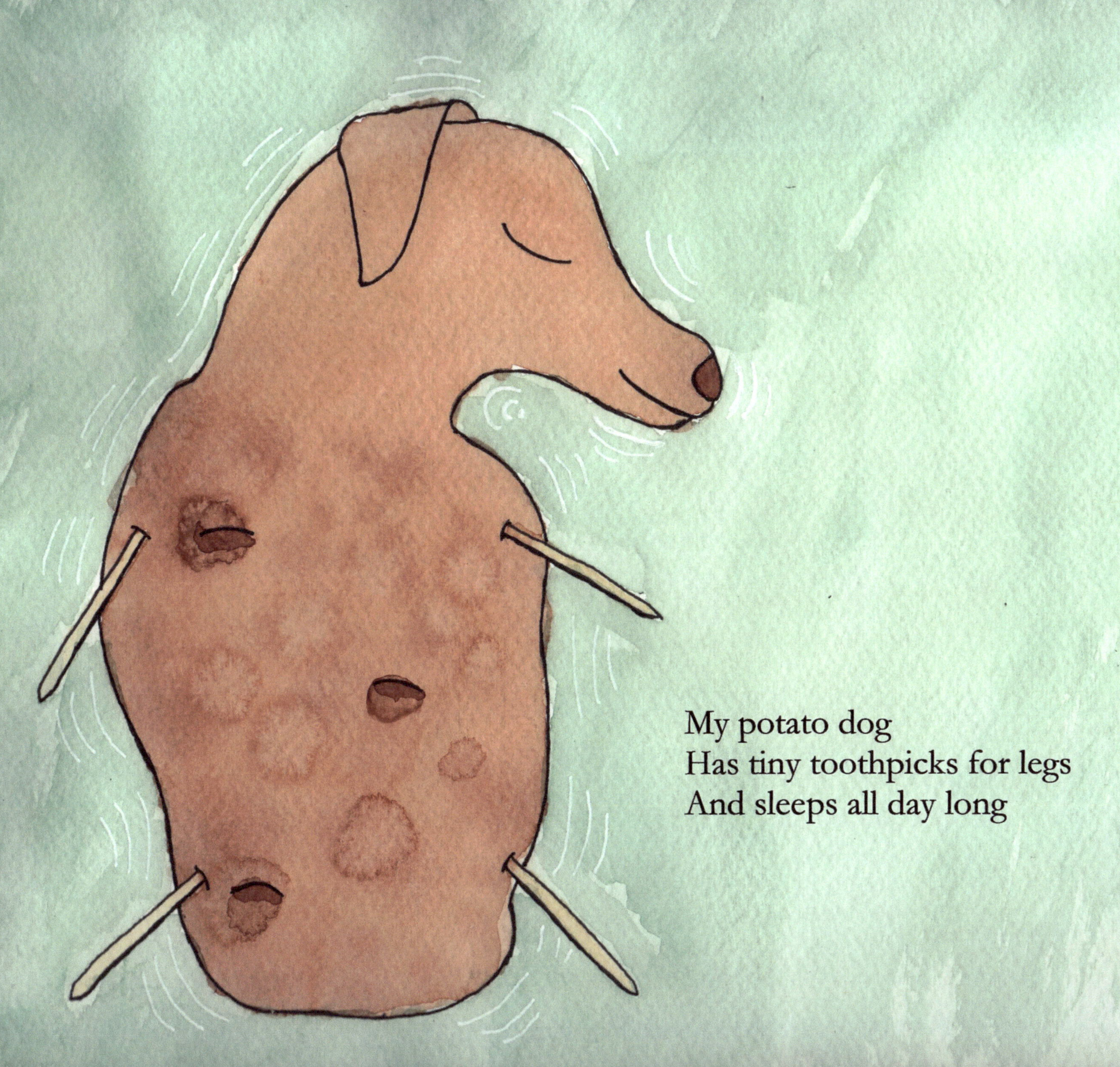

My potato dog
Has tiny toothpicks for legs
And sleeps all day long

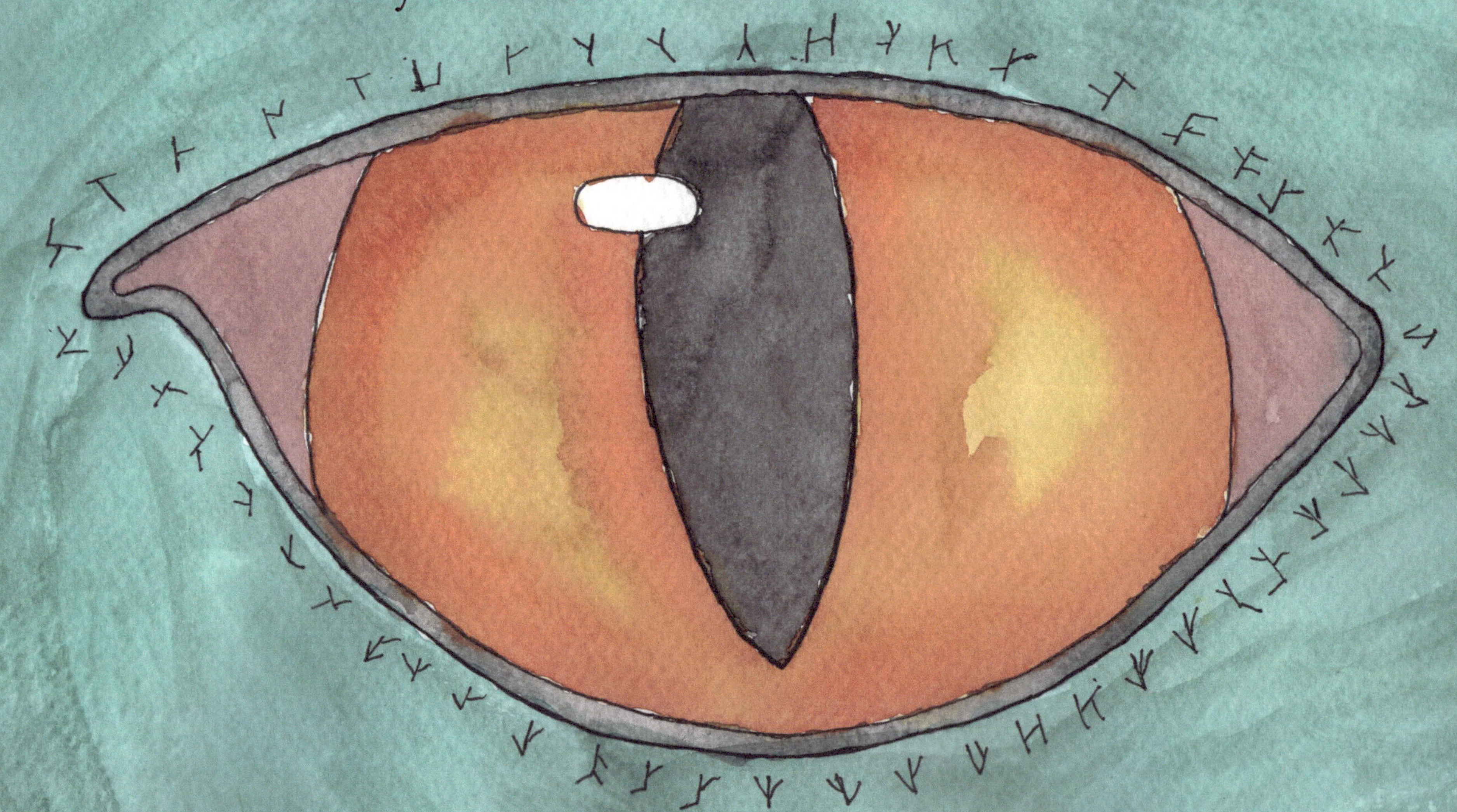

Eye of yon dragon
Tis beste ye avoide its gaize
Lest ye be eaten

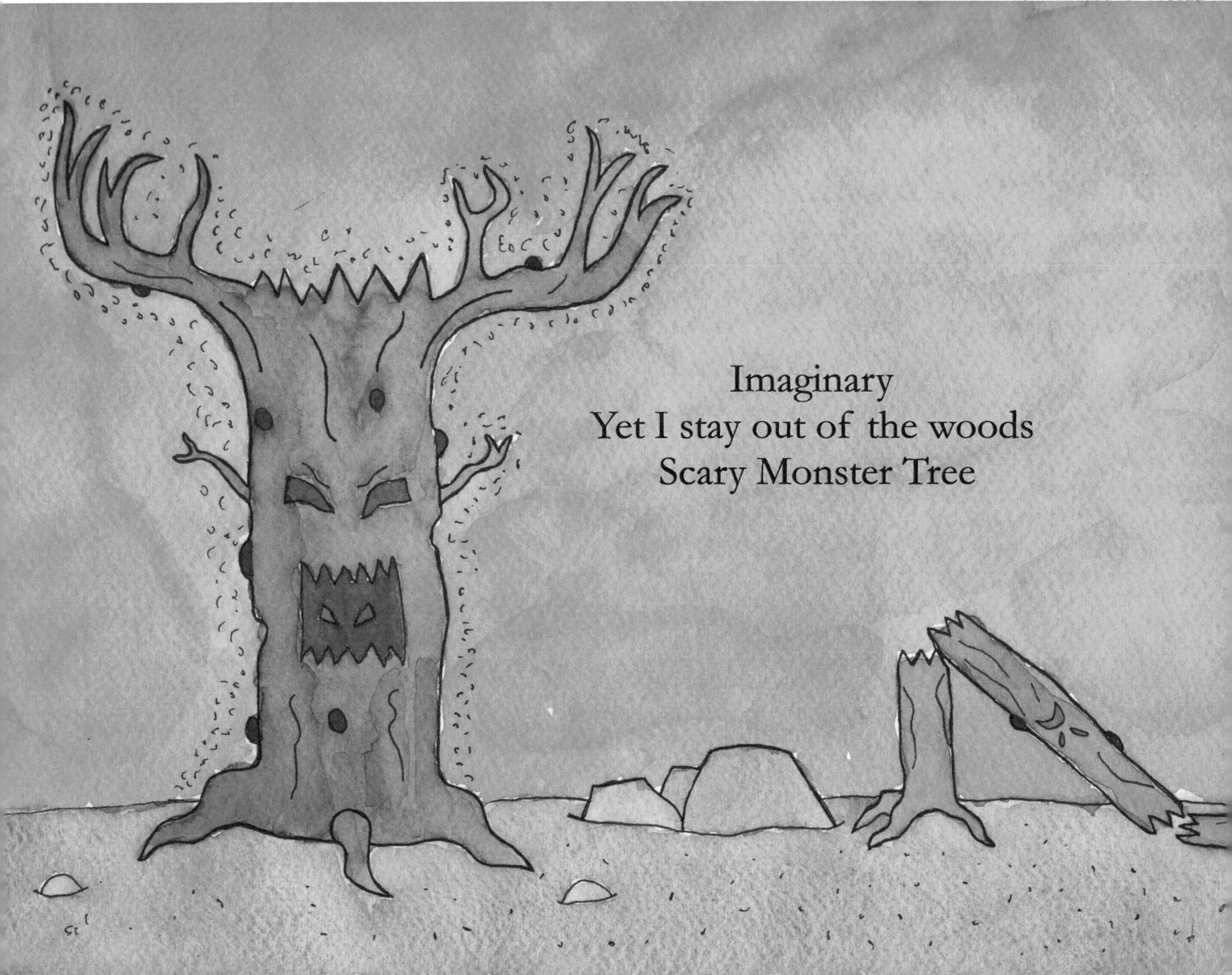

Imaginary
Yet I stay out of the woods
Scary Monster Tree

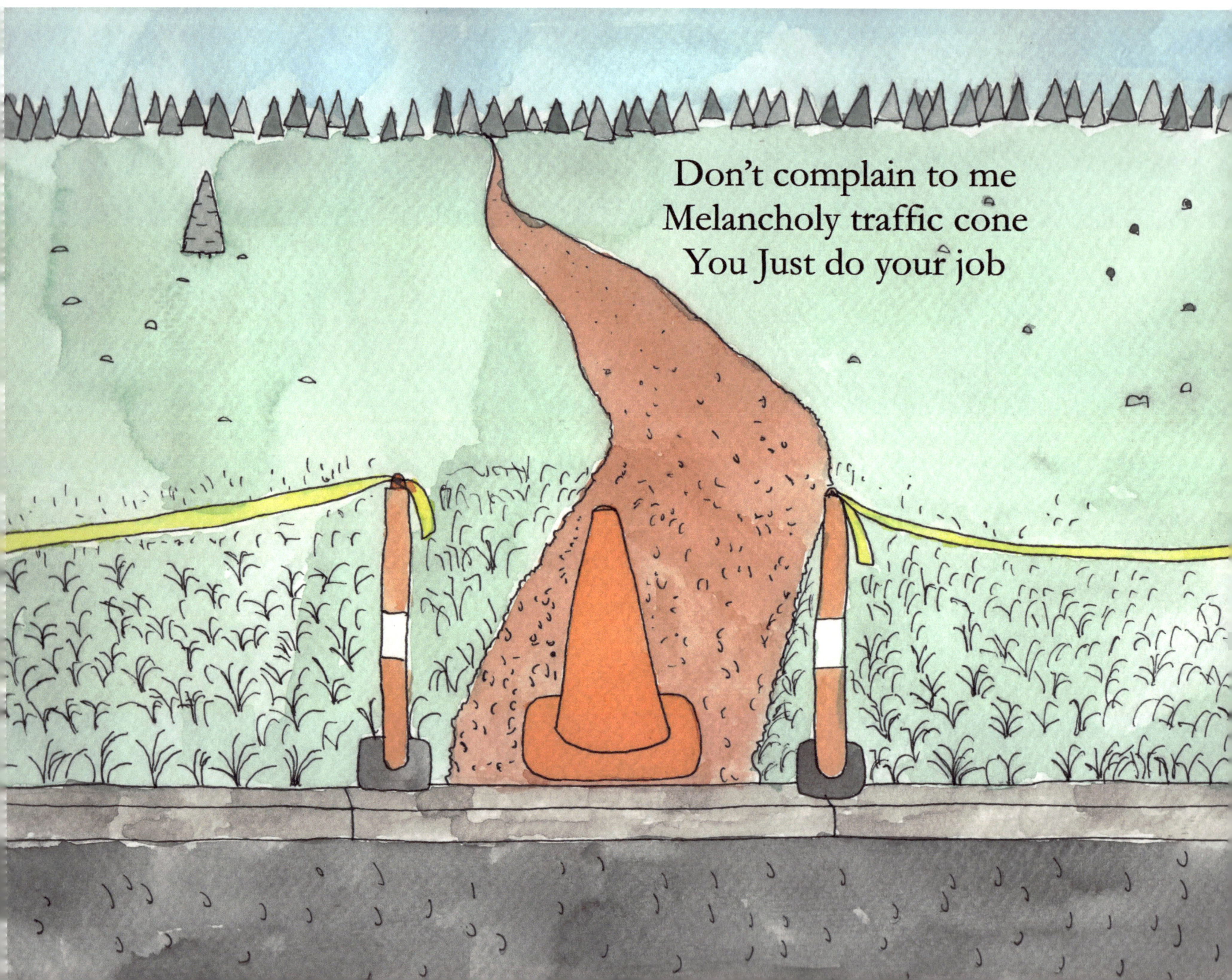

Don't complain to me
Melancholy traffic cone
You Just do your job

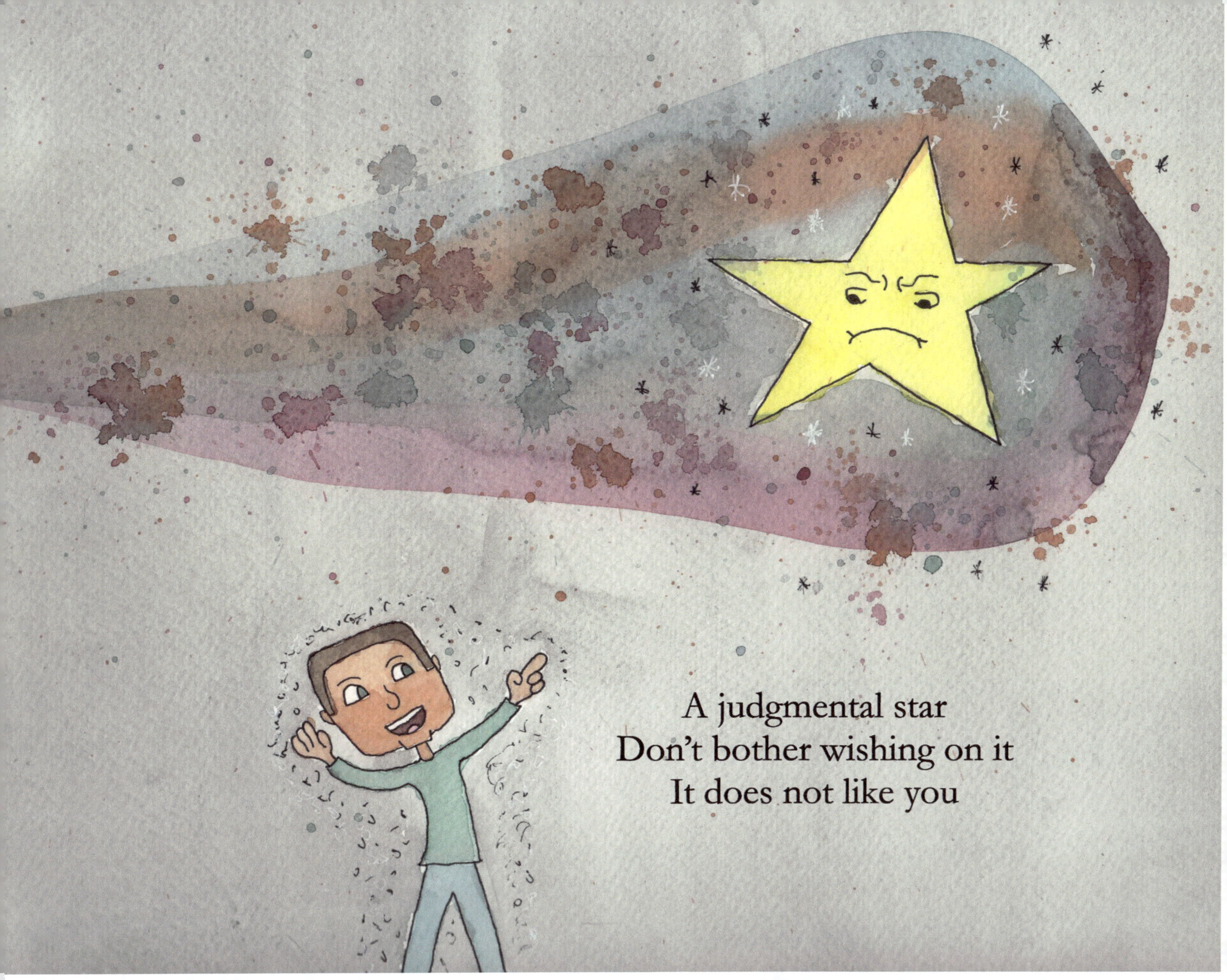

A judgmental star
Don't bother wishing on it
It does not like you

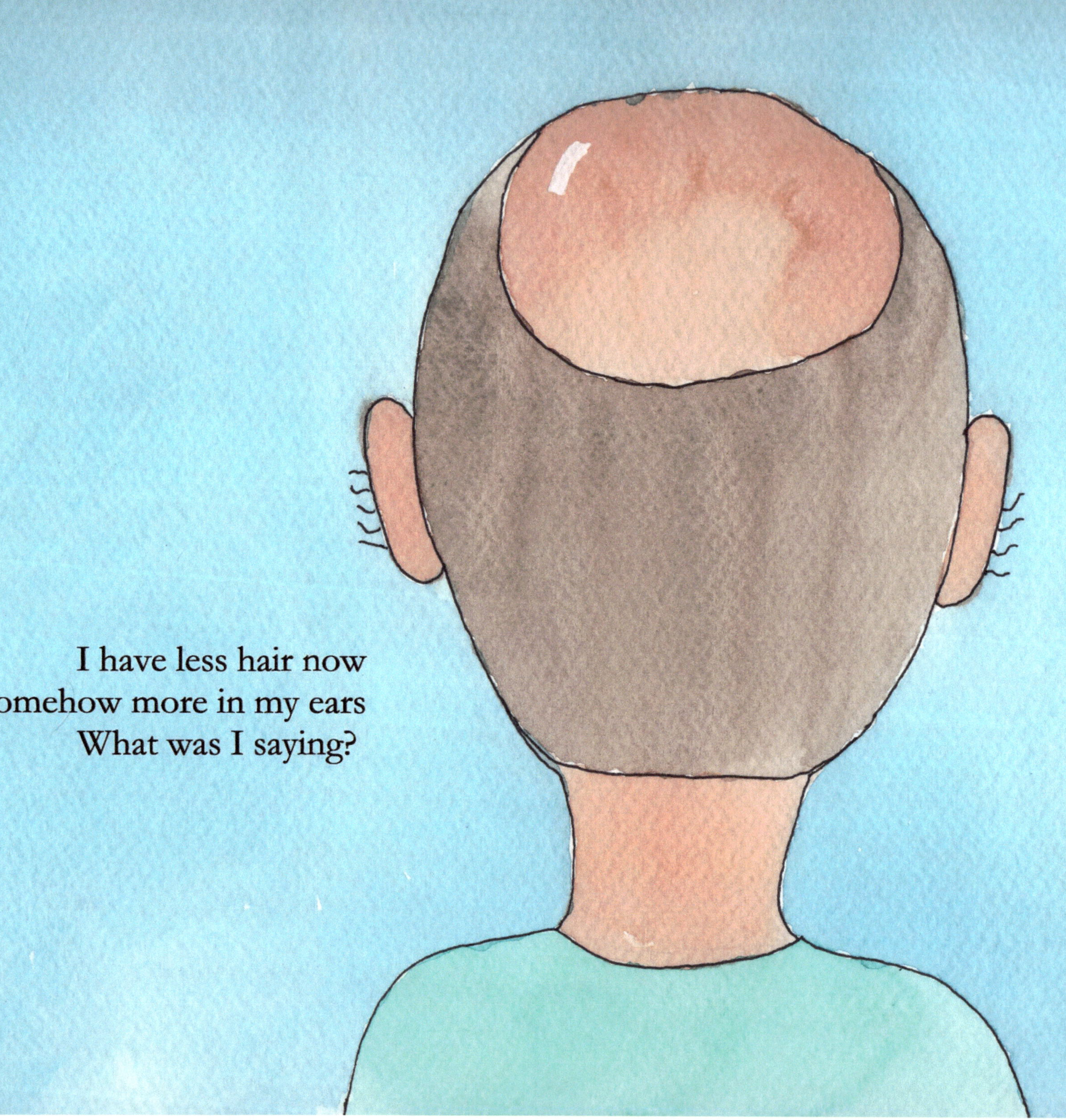

I have less hair now
But somehow more in my ears
What was I saying?

A runaway cart
Some new car's shiny bumper
Sure sucks for that guy

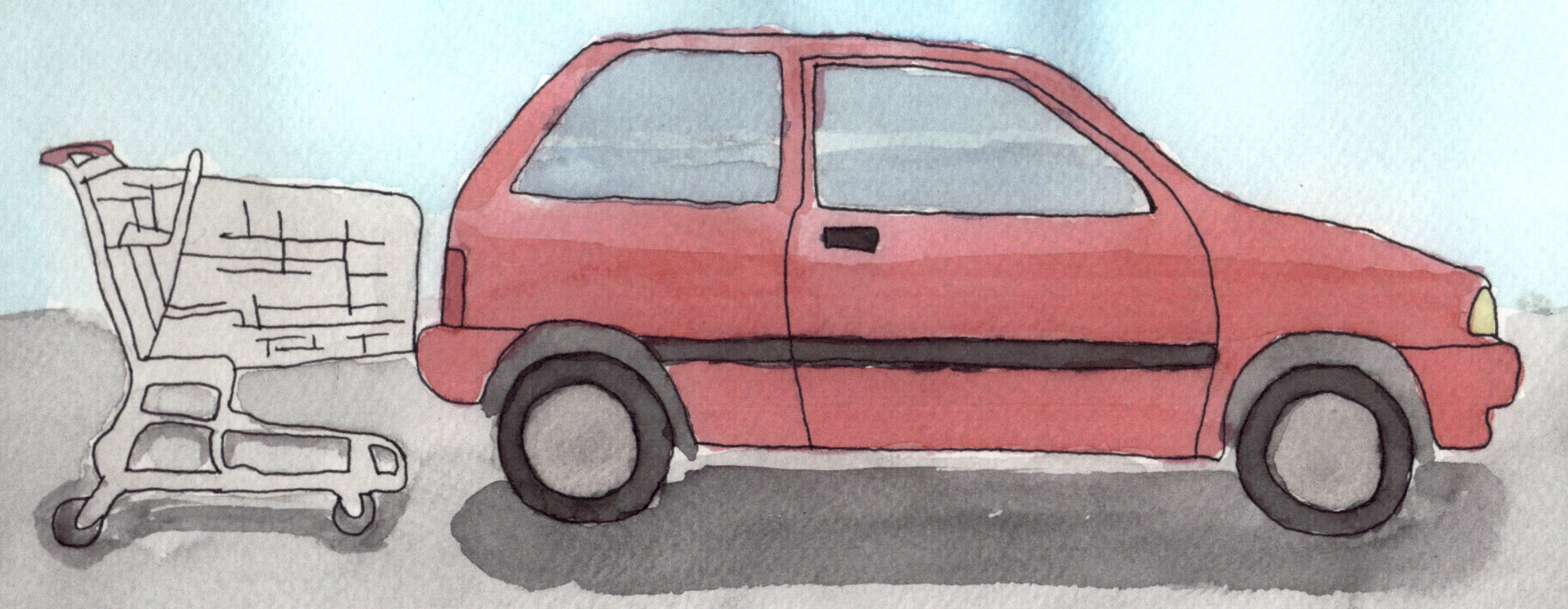

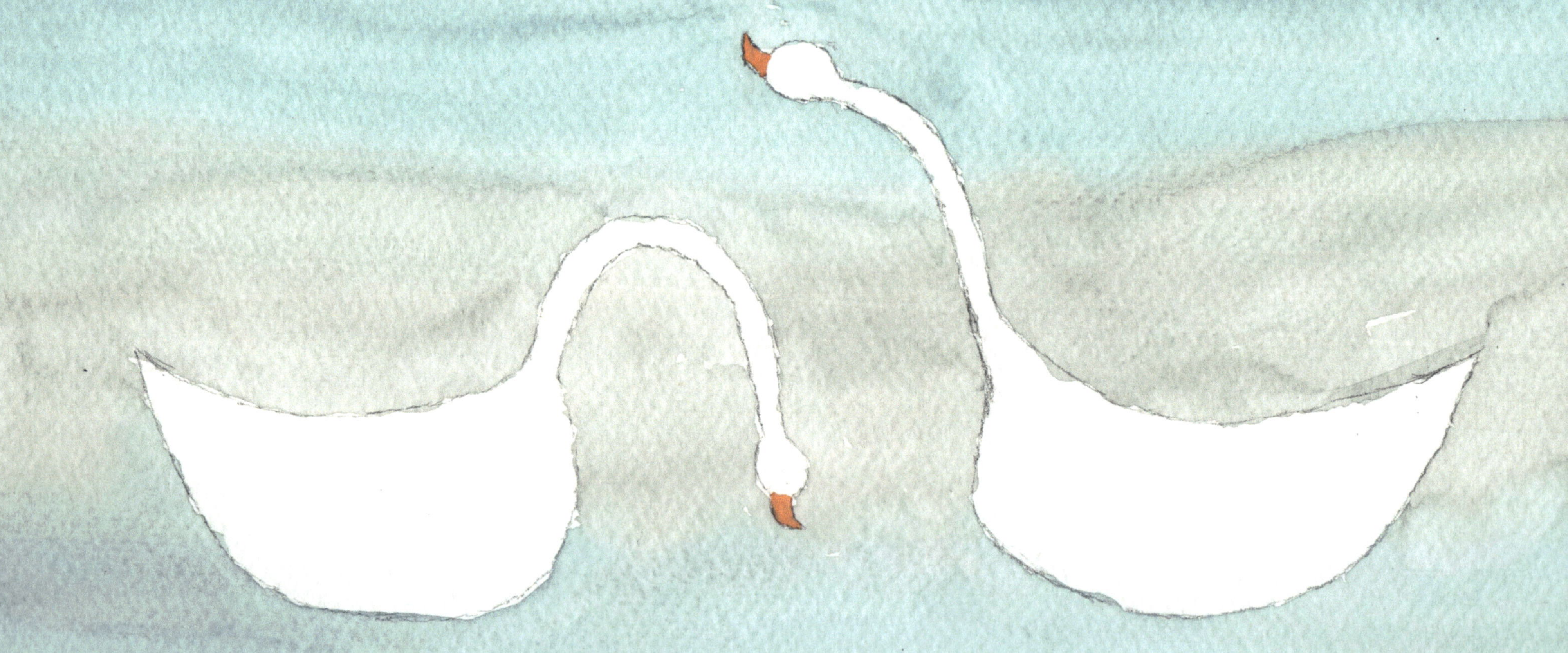

A ballet of swans
Butts in the air, necks held high
Ice on Lake Heron

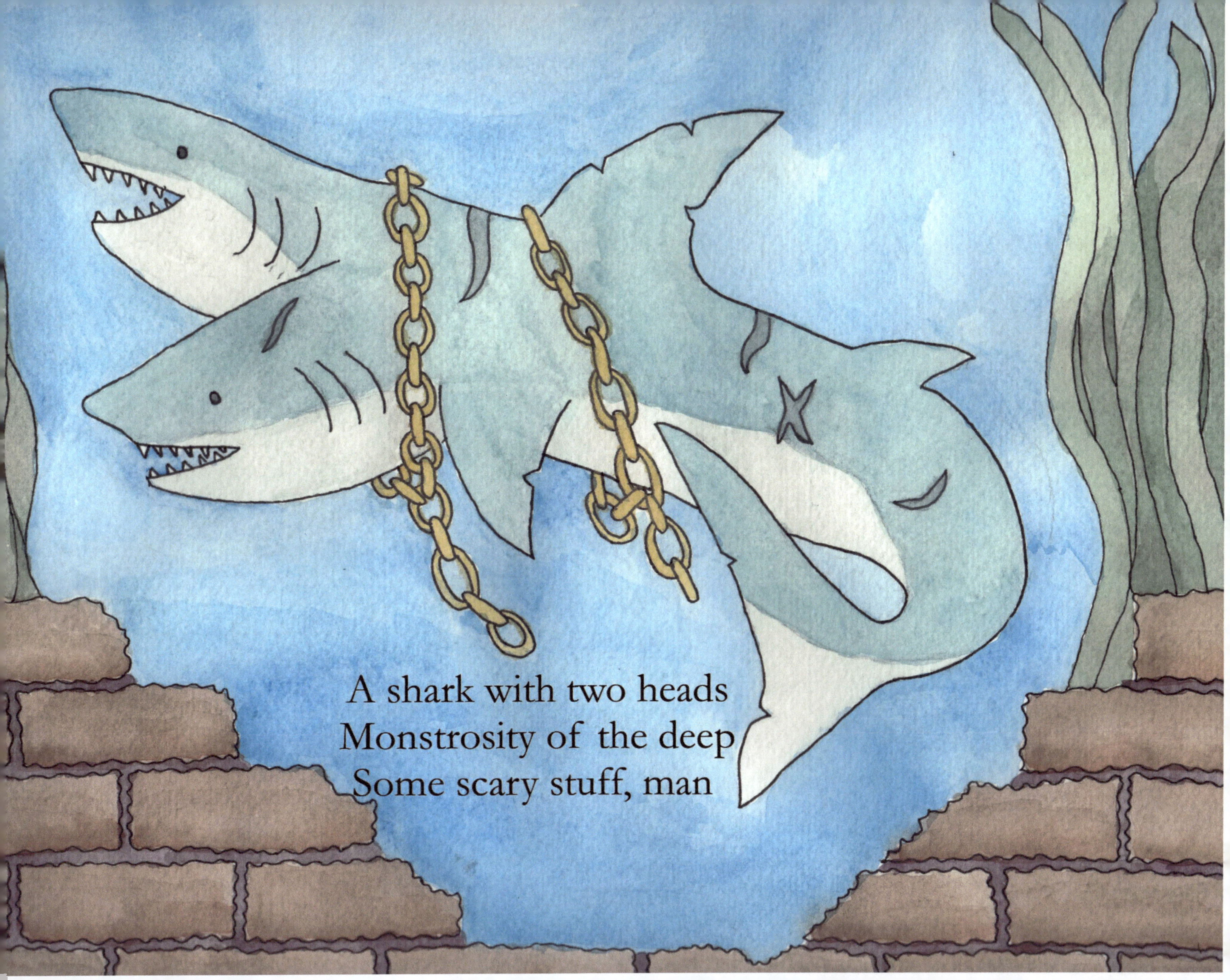
A shark with two heads
Monstrosity of the deep
Some scary stuff, man

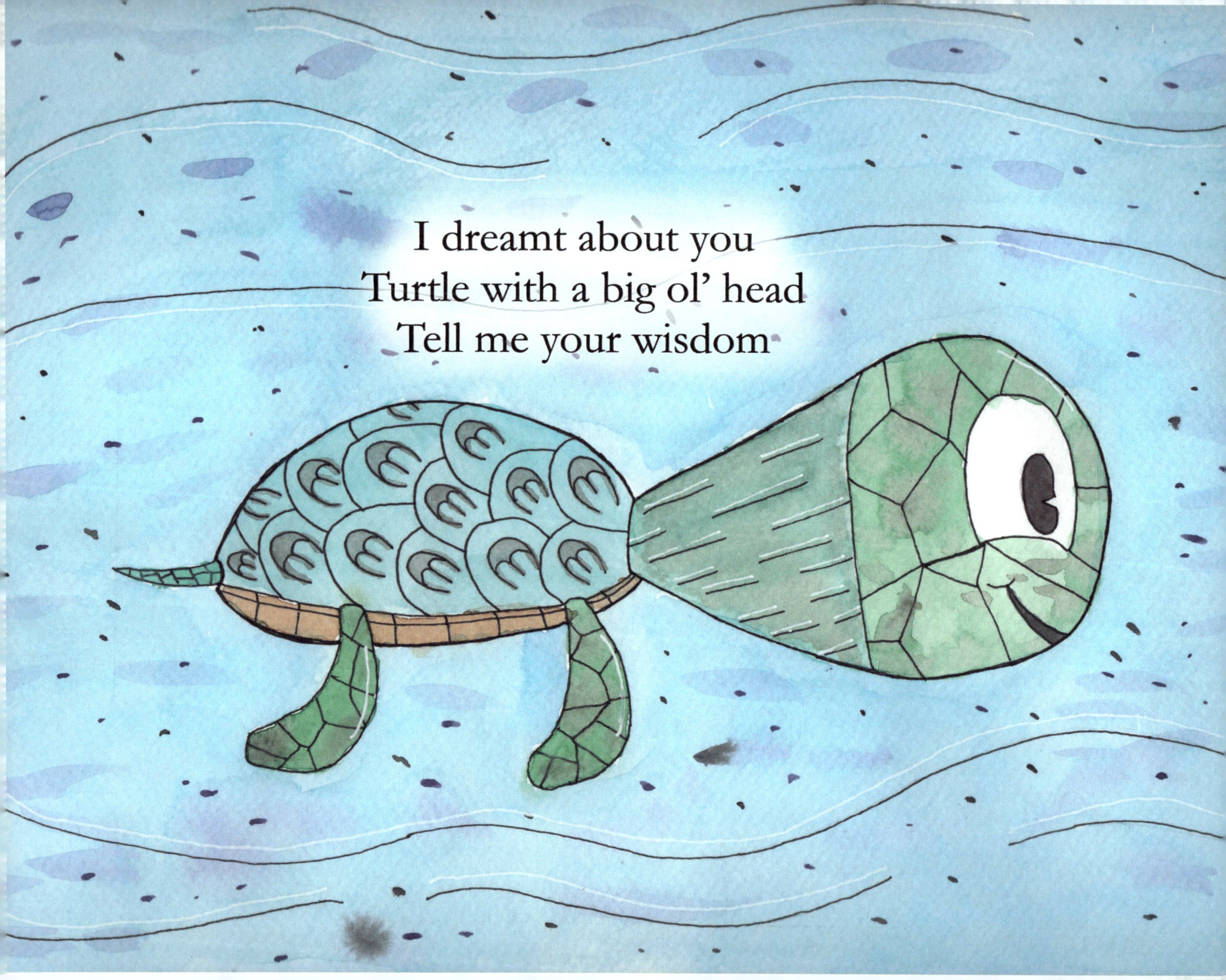

I dreamt about you
Turtle with a big ol' head
Tell me your wisdom

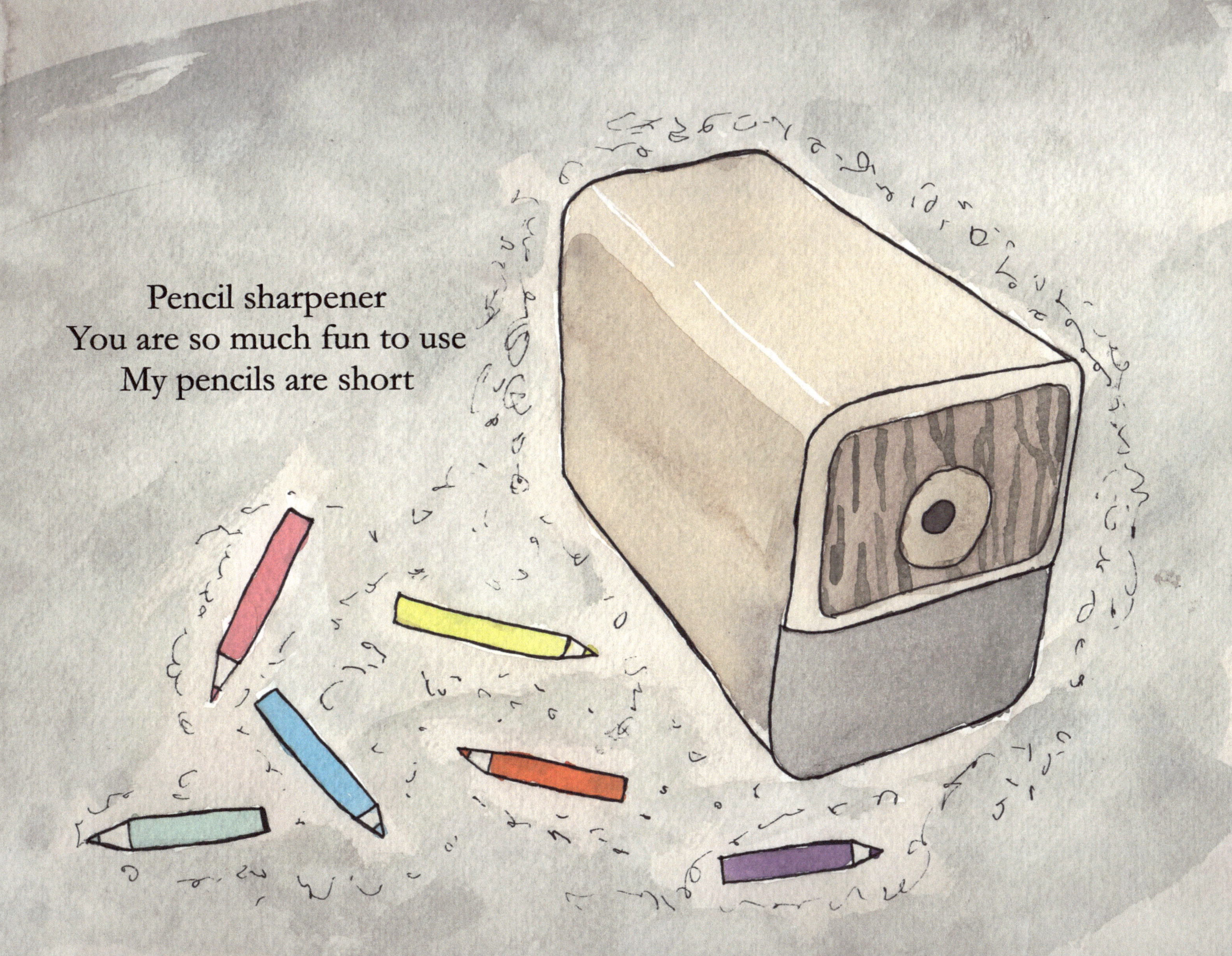

Pencil sharpener
You are so much fun to use
My pencils are short

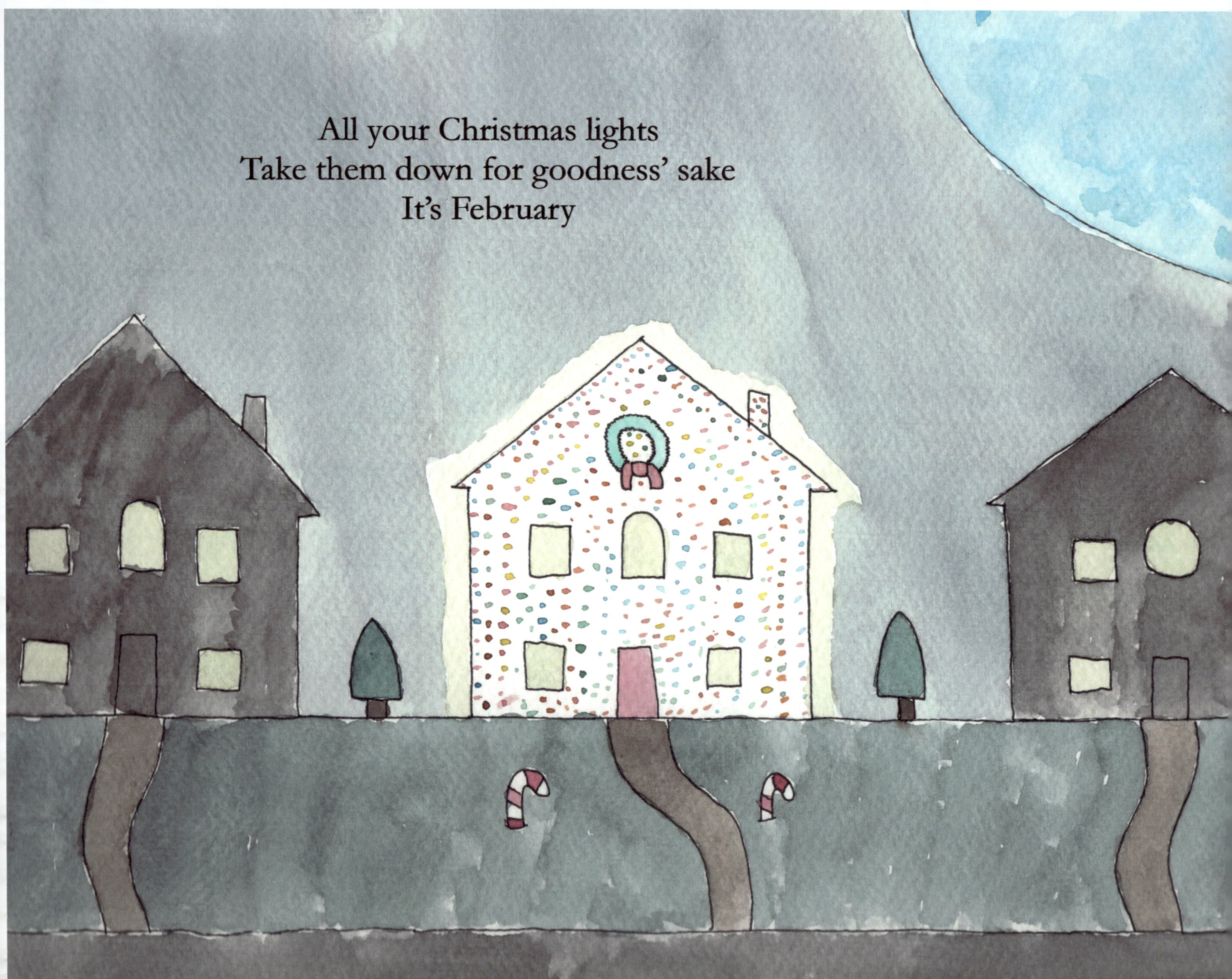
All your Christmas lights
Take them down for goodness' sake
It's February

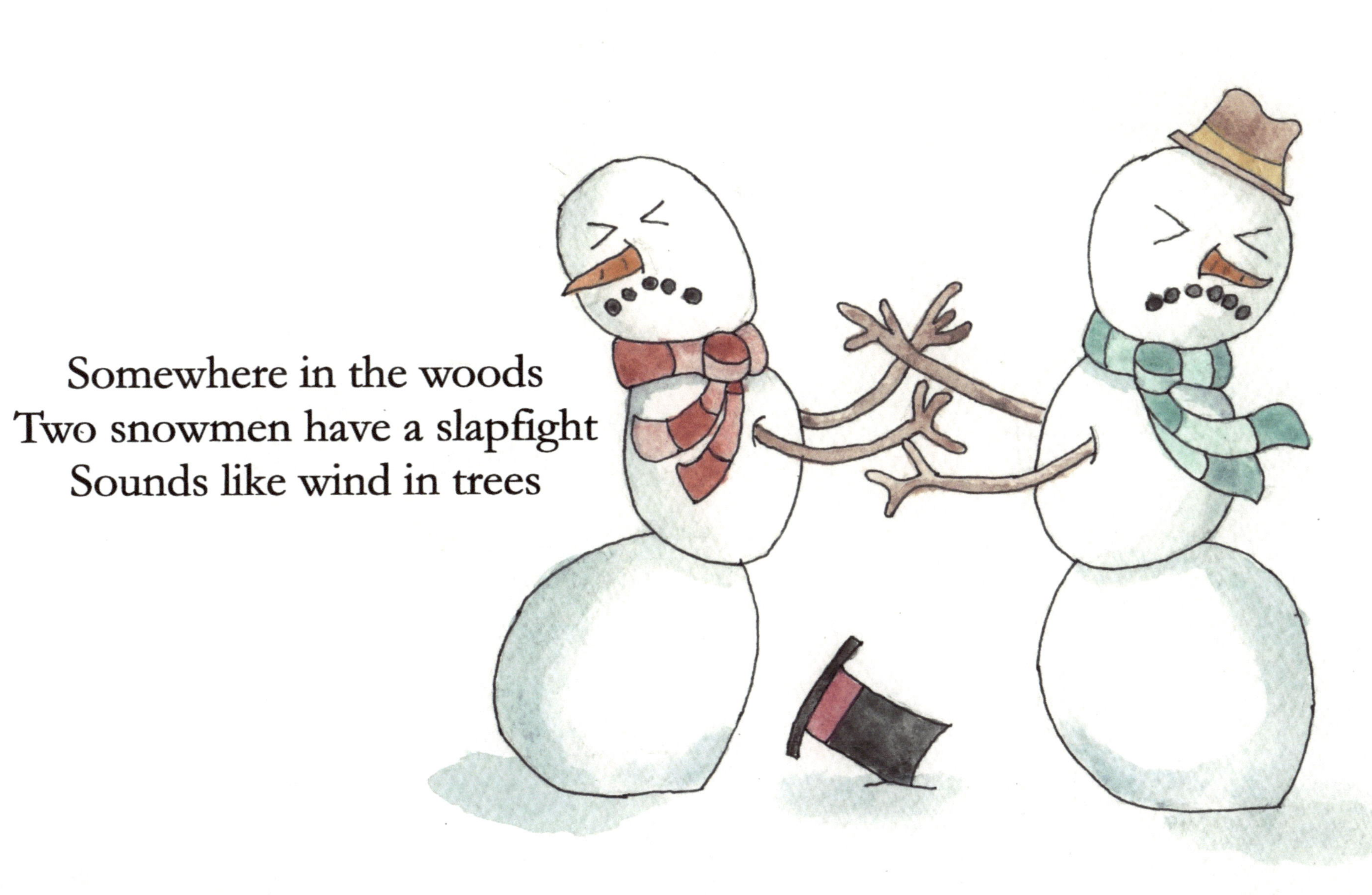

Somewhere in the woods
Two snowmen have a slapfight
Sounds like wind in trees

There are no fish here
But I sure do like the view
Said the fisherman

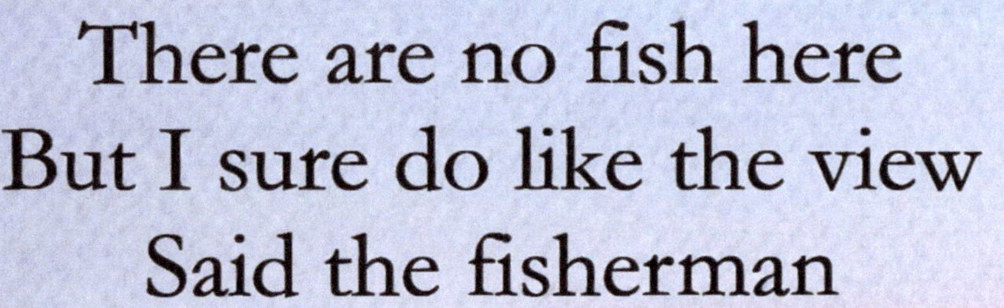

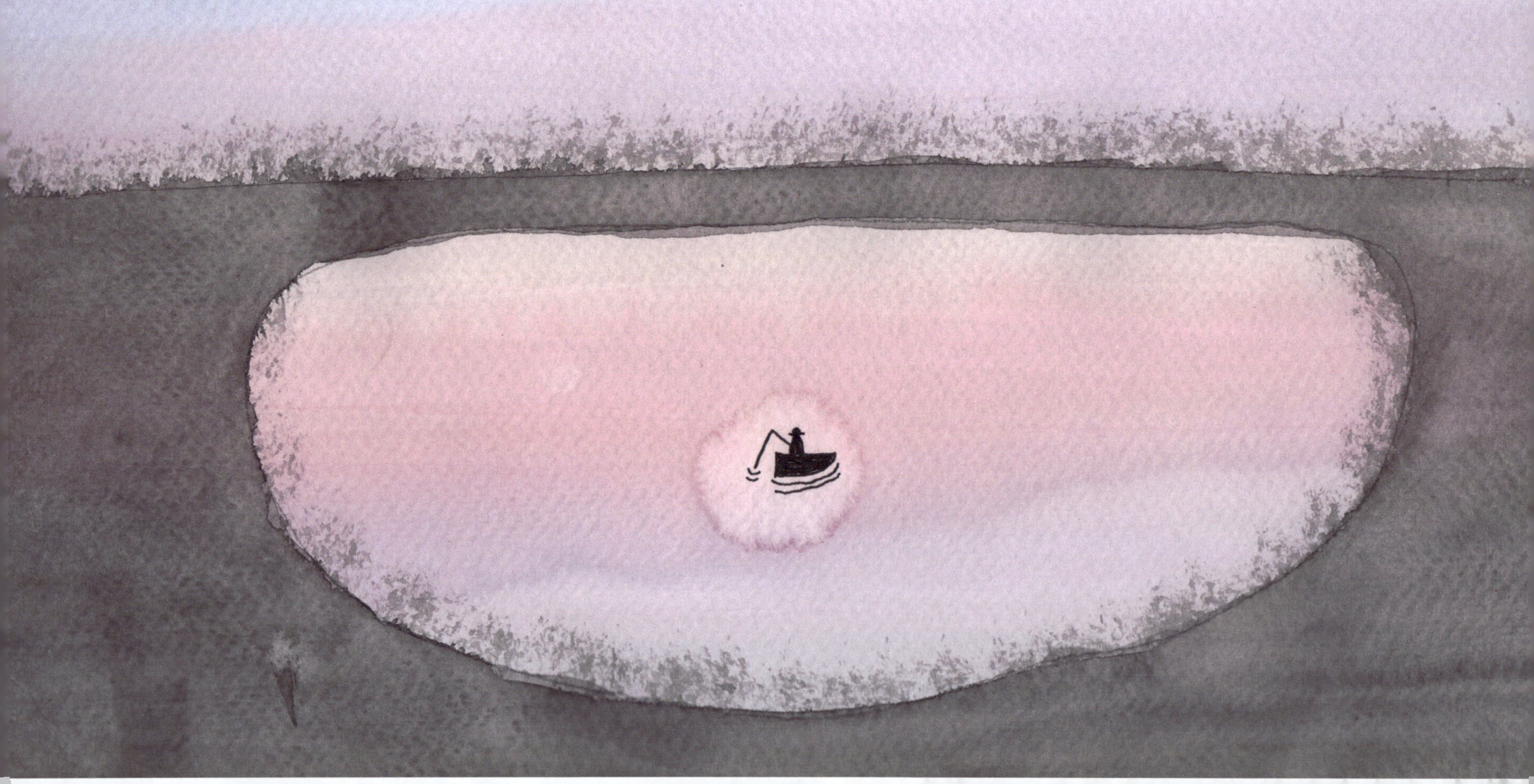

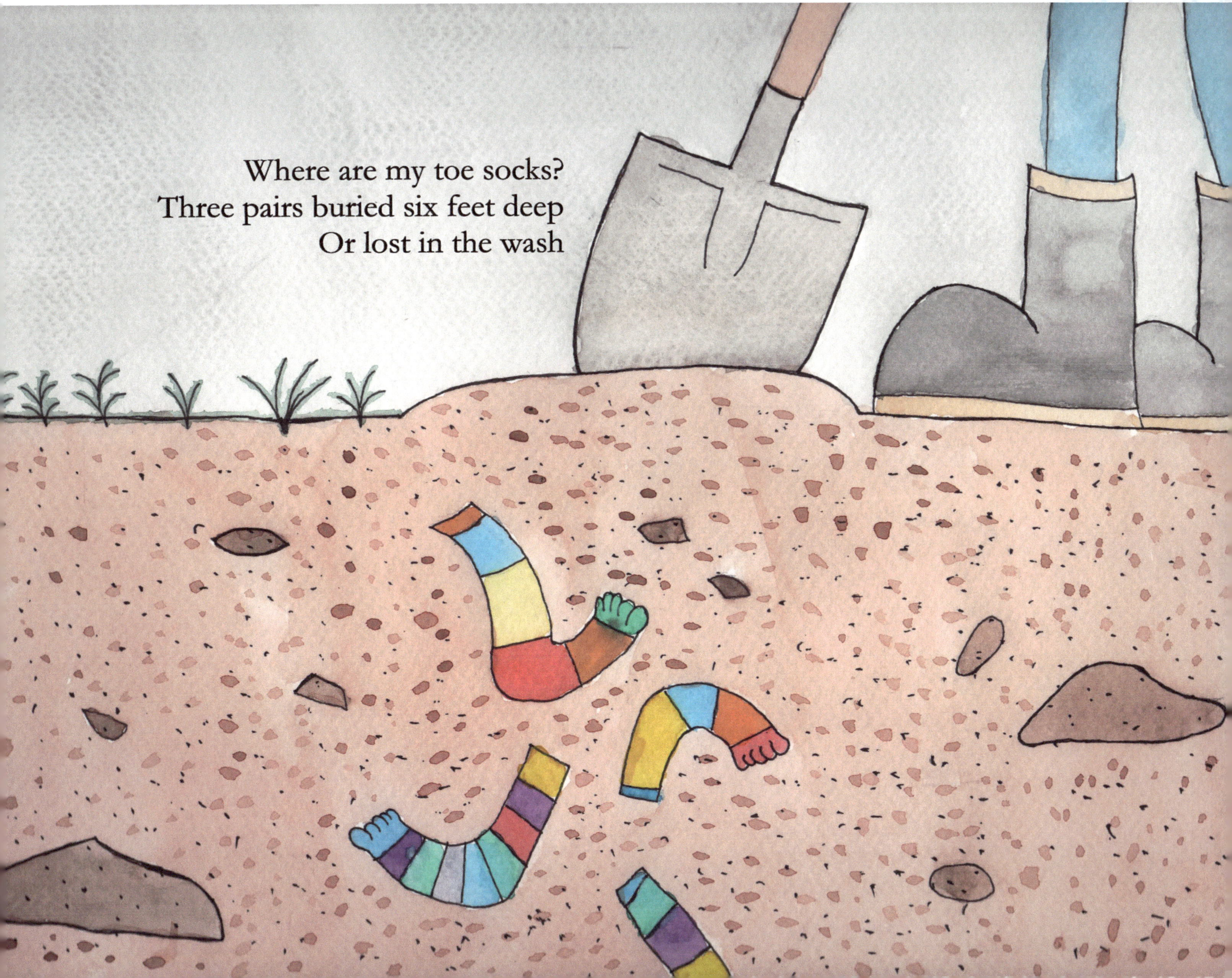

Where are my toe socks?
Three pairs buried six feet deep
Or lost in the wash

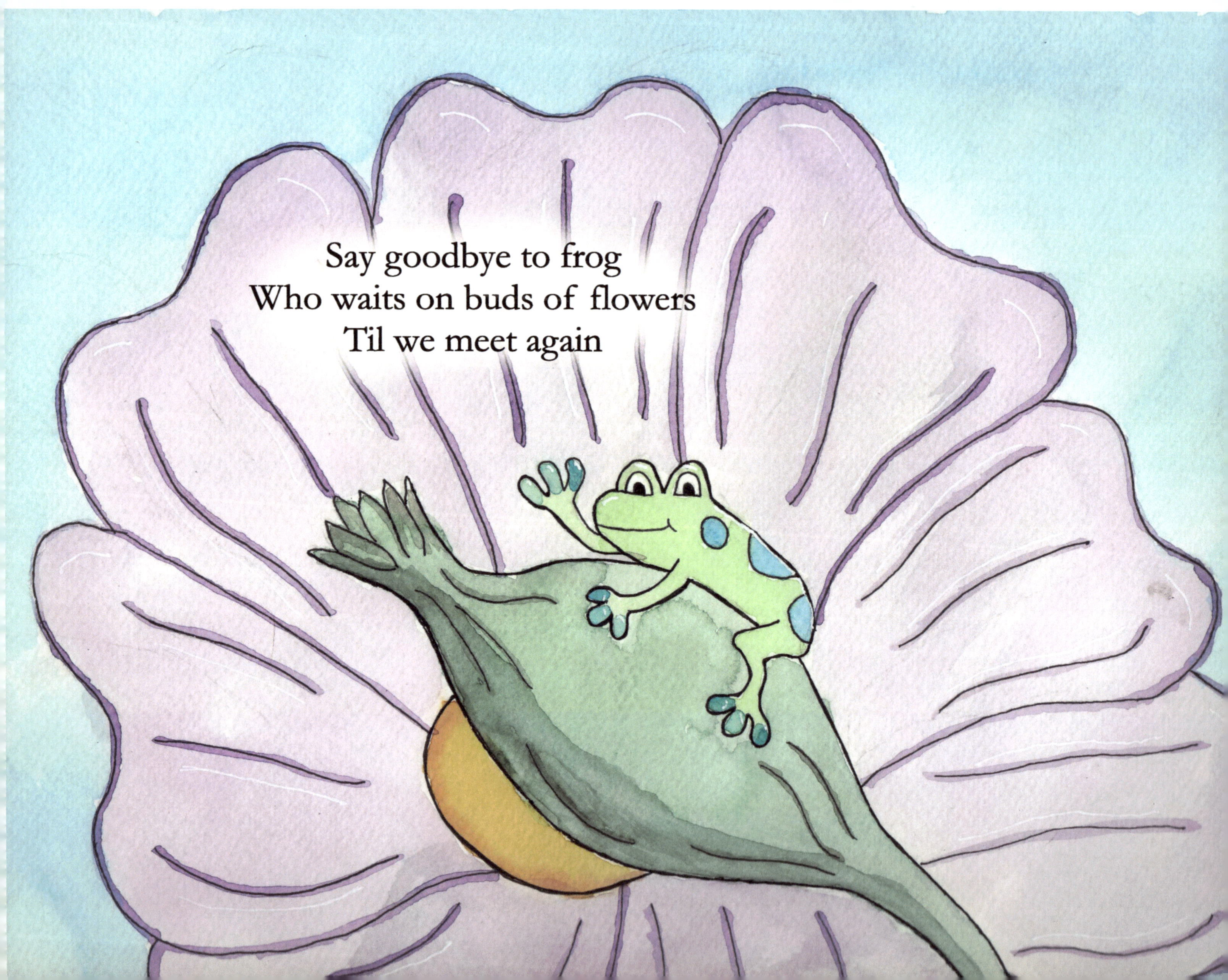
Say goodbye to frog
Who waits on buds of flowers
Til we meet again

www.ingramcontent.com/pod-product-compliance
Lightning Source LLC
Chambersburg PA
CBHW041034120726

48005CB00004B/803